THE 10

Most Amazing Birds

Jennifer Meghan Jenkins

Series Editor
Jeffrey D. Wilhelm

Much thought, debate, and research went into choosing and ranking the 10 items in each book in this series. We realize that everyone has his or her own opinion of what is most significant, revolutionary, amazing, deadly, and so on. As you read, you may agree with our choices, or you may be surprised — and that's the way it should be!

Rubicon © 2008 Rubicon Publishing Inc.
www.rubiconpublishing.com

 is a trademark of The 10 Books

Associate Publishers: Kim Koh, Miriam Bardswich
Project Editor: Amy Land
Editor: Bettina Fehrenbach
Creative Director: Jennifer Drew
Senior Designer: Jeanette MacLean
Graphic Designer: Rebecca Buchanan

The publisher gratefully acknowledges the following for permission to reprint copyrighted material in this book.

Every reasonable effort has been made to trace the owners of copyrighted material and to make due acknowledgment. Any errors or omissions drawn to our attention will be gladly rectified in future editions.

"The Bizarre Nesting Habits of the Hornbill" (excerpt) by David M. Bird, Ph.D. Professor of Wildlife Biology, McGill University. From *The Gazette*, April 24, 1993. Reprinted with permission.

"It's Great to Be Gross — Vultures Have Fun" (excerpt) by Claire Miller. Reprinted from the October 2001 issue of *Ranger Rick*® magazine, with the permission of the publisher, the National Wildlife Federation®.

"Does Rain Forest Bird 'Boom' Like a Dinosaur?" (excerpt) by James Owen. From *National Geographic News*, November 4, 2003. Reprinted with permission.

Cover: Egyptian vulture–Getty Images/Photographer's Choice/ 200397247-002

Library and Archives Canada Cataloguing in Publication

Jenkins, Meghan
    The 10 most amazing birds / Jennifer Meghan Jenkins.

Includes index.
ISBN 978-1-55448-532-1

    1. Readers (Elementary). 2. Readers—Birds. I. Title.
II. Title: Ten most amazing birds.

PE1117.J446 2007a   428.6   C2007-906693-3

2 3 4 5 6 7 8 9 10 11   24 23 22 21 20 19 18 17 16 17 16 15

Printed in Canada

Contents

Introduction: Prepare for Takeoff! 4

North Island Brown Kiwi 6
Is this actually a bird? Surprisingly, it is, and it's even a national mascot!

Sooty Shearwater 10
This bird has shattered records no other bird can compete with.

Peregrine Falcon 14
Prey better run for cover when this fast flier comes around.

Secretary Bird 18
This bird has a kick that will knock you unconscious, or dead …

Great Hornbill 22
How many uses can a large bill have? Find out from the great hornbill!

Egyptian Vulture 26
If roadkill is on the menu, this bird will say, "Yum!"

Ostrich 30
This bird may look awkward, but it will outrun you and most other creatures!

Ruby-Throated Hummingbird 34
Get this bird a chill pill! Everything it does is fast.

Cassowary 38
This bird gives us an idea of what a dinosaur might have sounded like.

Emperor Penguin 42
Penguins must love the cold to live in these extreme temperatures!

We Thought … 46

What Do You Think? 47

Index 48

18

26

42

PREPARE FOR TAKEOFF!

When you think of a bird, what comes to mind? Wings? Beaks? Endless flights in the sky? Part of that description is accurate; however, you'll be surprised to know that not all birds fly. There are so many different types of birds that it's hard to believe that they can all be called birds! While many do fly, others prefer to walk, run, or swim. Some eat meat, while others stick to fruits and veggies. Some birds don't even look like birds at all!

Ornithologists — scientists who study birds — have the fun job of watching and learning from these interesting creatures. Ornithologists have learned that the behavior of birds can give us answers about the health of our environment.

Birds alert us to changes in the weather and how to make use of the materials around us. Through their adaptations, they can even show us how to survive! All in all, birds are pretty amazing. You won't believe the tricks some of these birds have hiding up their wings! It's no wonder there are so many enthusiastic birdwatchers in the world.

In this book we present the 10 birds we think are the most amazing. We ranked them based on their special features, their unique habits, and the amazing things they do to survive in their habitats. Read about these unbelievable winged creatures, and ask yourself:

WHAT IS THE MOST AMAZING BIRD IN THE WORLD?

The kiwi has an extraordinary sense of smell because of the nostrils near the tip of its bill.

BROWN KIWI

HEIGHT: 20 in. (females are slightly larger)

WEIGHT: 3.3 to 7.9 lb.

WOW FACTOR: This strange little creature is so unlike any other bird in the world that many people consider it to be an honorary mammal!

Whatever you know about other birds, forget it! The kiwi breaks all of the rules. It can't fly, it doesn't have amazing eyesight, it doesn't build the best nests, and it doesn't have the longest wings. In fact, if it didn't have feathers and a beak, you probably wouldn't think it was a bird at all!

However, despite these surprising details, the North Island brown kiwi is amazing in other ways. Aside from being New Zealand's national mascot, the kiwi has a great sense of smell. It may not have long legs, but it will walk all night looking for food.

The North Island brown kiwi is special and unique for many reasons. Turn the page to see what else makes this bird amazing.

NORTH ISLAND BROWN KIWI

BIRD WATCH

You wouldn't be alone in mistaking the kiwi for a small rodent! The kiwi is shaped like a pear, with a small head, a large behind, and no tail feathers. Its brown plumage is streaked with black, and its loose, shaggy feathers look like the soft, fur coat of a mammal. It has very tiny eyes and a long slender bill. The kiwi is the only bird in the world that has nostrils at the end of its bill, rather than at the base. The kiwi's bill can be up to eight inches long!

WHAT'S FOR DINNER?

The kiwi has a varied diet that includes beetles, snails, crayfish, fruits, berries, earthworms, and insects. The kiwi is a predatory bird that uses its sense of smell and hearing to locate food. It plunges its long beak into the dirt and leaf litter on the forest floor to find its food. The kiwi usually hunts at night.

plumage: *feathers around a bird's body*
predatory: *describing animals that kill and eat other animals*

? The kiwi doesn't fly, so how has it adapted to survive on land? Explain.

The Expert Says...

" Whatever you know about other birds, throw it out the window. Kiwis are very different. They lay eggs and have feathers, and other than that, they just aren't like other birds. "

— Kathy Brader, senior bird keeper, National Zoological Park, Washington, D.C.

NO-FLIGHT ZONE

New Zealand consists of two large islands — North Island and South Island — as well as smaller islands where all five species of the kiwi can be found. The North Island brown kiwi makes its home just where its name suggests: on the North Island! Its original habitat was coniferous forests, but most of this has been cleared by people as they move to the area. Now the kiwi has been forced to adapt to life on farmland and partially cleared forests. A kiwi's home territory can be as big as 124 acres, and the small bird can travel that entire distance in a single night.

coniferous: *relating to trees bearing evergreen leaves and cones*

? Why do you think the kiwi is losing its habitat? What can you do to help stop this?

Quick Fact

The kiwi builds numerous tunnels underneath the ground, with large burrows at the end where it sleeps during the day.

The kiwi has whiskers, like a mammal, to help it find its way around in the dark.

10 9 8 7 6

THE INCREDIBLE KIWI

Aww! This North Island brown kiwi is only one week old.

The kiwi's legs and feet are extremely strong. They are so important to the bird's survival that they account for about one third of the bird's total weight!

? Considering where kiwis live, why is it important for them to have such strong feet and legs?

Kiwi birds lay very large eggs for their size. While an ostrich egg is big, it is only about 1.7 percent of the ostrich's body weight. A kiwi egg is about 25 percent of the kiwi's entire body weight!

The kiwi gets its name from the shrill whistling call that male kiwis use to communicate with other kiwis. Kiwis are extremely noisy birds, constantly grunting, growling, hissing, and snuffling while looking for food.

Kiwis are very territorial and will fight off anything that comes too close. The kiwi grabs an intruder with its beak to hold it still. Then it kicks at the intruder with its strong, scaly legs and sharp claws.

Unlike most chicks, which use their beaks to break out of their shells, kiwi chicks actually kick their way out with their powerful legs.

Take Note

The kiwi is #10 on our list of amazing birds because it is a unique bird with physical characteristics and traits that set it apart from all of the other birds on this list.
• Do you agree that being unique is amazing? Are you impressed by the kiwi? Why or why not?

Sooty shearwaters increase their body mass by around 40 percent before their flight across the Pacific Ocean.

WATER

LENGTH: 15.7 to 19.7 in.

WINGSPAN: 37 to 43 in.

WOW FACTOR: Pack your bags! This bird holds the longest migration record of all birds — and even all animals!

That old saying, "never judge a book by its cover," certainly holds true for this little bird. We didn't think that there was anything amazing about the sooty shearwater. Then we found out that there are more important things in life than looks!

The sooty shearwater surprised us all when scientists found out that this unassuming bird migrates the farthest of all birds. Until recently, it was believed that the Arctic tern had the longest migration. However, scientists tagged the sooty shearwater and realized this soot-colored bird travels a lot farther. The average distance covered by the sooty shearwater in a year is about 33,550 miles. Some have been recorded to travel as far as 46,000 miles! These birds spend about 90 percent of their lives in the air. They only come down to breed and nest.

The sooty shearwater has ornithologists all around the world buzzing with excitement … and with good reason. This bird doesn't need bright feathers or large wings to stand out in a crowd.

SOOTY SHEARWATER

BIRD WATCH

The sooty shearwater gets its name from the color of its feathers. Some people think this bird looks dirty, as though it has been rolling around in a pile of soot. It has brown feathers that are darkest on the tips of its wings. The sooty is a strong, stocky bird, almost as big as a mallard duck, but more streamlined like a falcon. Both males and females have dark bodies with silver and white lining underneath their wings. The sooty's upper bill is hooked to help it catch and eat fish.

WHAT'S FOR DINNER?

This bird is a real fan of seafood, including small fish, squid, shrimp-like krill, and jellyfish. As sooty shearwaters fly over the water, they have a bird's-eye view of their prey, especially when close to the surface. When it spots a tasty fish, it plunges into the ocean, using its powerful wings to dive under water.

FLIGHT ZONE

A world traveler, the sooty shearwater covers a lot of miles. It nests in various locations in the Southern Hemisphere, including New Zealand and Chile. Then it heads to feeding grounds in the Northern Hemisphere near Japan, Alaska, and California. And the sooty shearwater doesn't always follow its family members — it can head to a completely different country.

? Sooties are small birds, yet they migrate long distances. How are they equipped to do this? Do some research to find out.

The Expert Says...

" These extraordinary migration routes represent the longest recorded of any animal tracked to date. The only other bird species that could rival the migrations of the sooty shearwater would be the Arctic tern. "

— Dr. Scott Shaffer, research biologist at the University of California

When hunting, sooty shearwaters typically dive about 46 feet to catch their prey. They have been known to dive as deep as 230 feet!

10   **9**   **8**   **7**   **6**

What A Trip!

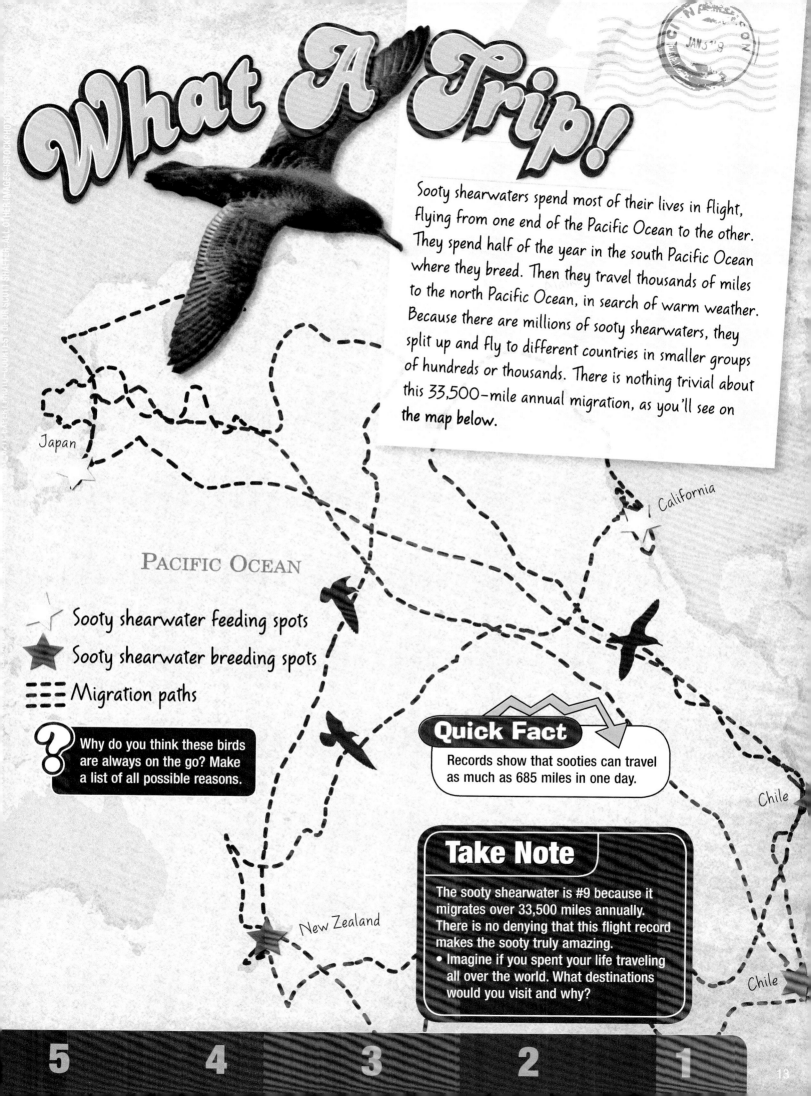

Sooty shearwaters spend most of their lives in flight, flying from one end of the Pacific Ocean to the other. They spend half of the year in the south Pacific Ocean where they breed. Then they travel thousands of miles to the north Pacific Ocean, in search of warm weather. Because there are millions of sooty shearwaters, they split up and fly to different countries in smaller groups of hundreds or thousands. There is nothing trivial about this 33,500-mile annual migration, as you'll see on the map below.

Japan

PACIFIC OCEAN

California

⭐ Sooty shearwater feeding spots

★ Sooty shearwater breeding spots

▄▄▄ Migration paths

? Why do you think these birds are always on the go? Make a list of all possible reasons.

Quick Fact

Records show that sooties can travel as much as 685 miles in one day.

Chile

New Zealand

Take Note

The sooty shearwater is #9 because it migrates over 33,500 miles annually. There is no denying that this flight record makes the sooty truly amazing.
• Imagine if you spent your life traveling all over the world. What destinations would you visit and why?

Chile

5   4   3   2   1

Back off — get your own lunch! Peregrine falcons love their meat.

FALCON

LENGTH: Between 1 and 2 ft.

WINGSPAN: 3 ft.

WOW FACTOR: This bird is ace of the fly-by killing. With its incredible speed, most of its victims don't even know what hit them!

You probably enjoy watching the birds in your neighborhood. They peck on seeds and berries and munch on gooey insects and earthworms. They chirp happily in the trees. But if a peregrine (per-i-grin) falcon lands near you — watch out!

With its powerful wings and a streamlined body, the peregrine falcon is one of the fastest birds in the skies. No prey can hope to hide from the peregrine falcon's excellent eyesight — it can see six times better than a human being! The peregrine falcon's weapons of choice are a sharp, hooked bill and vicious talons that can tear flesh from bones. Add to that a love of raw meat, and you have a perfectly built killing machine!

Wondering if you should run for cover at the mere sight of this bird? Well, turn the page to find out what the peregrine falcon considers a tasty snack.

PEREGRINE FALCON

BIRD WATCH

An attractive bird, the peregrine falcon has slate-blue feathers on its back and wings. Its underside ranges from white to pale yellow and is often marked with dark brown or black spots and bars. With a black head and a yellow ring around its eyes, it looks as though this bird is wearing a helmet. The black under the bird's eyes absorbs light and reduces glare, helping the bird to see better.

WHAT'S FOR DINNER?

The peregrine falcon is a master hunter. It uses its incredible eyesight to stalk its prey from high above and dives in for the kill! This bird is not a picky eater. Ornithologists have observed it eating more than 100 different bird species, as well as small mammals, frogs, and even insects. Small prey are not safe when this bird is on the prowl!

What are the benefits or drawbacks of having such a varied diet?

FLIGHT ZONE

This hungry predator can be found all around the world, with the exception of Antarctica, New Zealand, and Iceland. Like the sooty shearwater, the peregrine falcon doesn't like to stay in one place for too long. In fact, the name "peregrine" comes from the Latin word *peregrinus*, which means wanderer.

Quick Fact

The peregrine falcon was on the Endangered Species List in the 1960s. The reason that the falcon population dramatically declined was because it was poisoned by a pesticide called DDT. DDT was in the plants that small animals and birds ate. In turn, the falcon ate these prey and absorbed the deadly pesticide. When DDT was banned, the birds made a major comeback and were removed from the list in 1999.

The Expert Says...

" They're real survivors. You know, they've survived this tremendous chemical impact that we subjected them to. It's a wildlife success story. I mean, we've been able to pull them back from the brink of extinction — we've been able to correct a terrible mistake that human beings are responsible for. "

— Phil Trefry, falcon breeder

ZOOMING in for the kill

Want to know more amazing facts about the peregrine falcon? Read the descriptive account below!

The peregrine falcon has mastered the surprise attack. Hunting in open fields, near mountains, along seacoasts, and even in large cities, it flies high above the ground looking for its next victim. When it spots a tasty treat, the falcon folds its tail feathers together in a streamlined shape and performs a near-vertical dive, plummeting toward the ground. Attacking from heights of a mile, the bird ends its dive-bomb attack by striking its prey with its powerful talons. The falcon then either drops its prey and follows it to the ground, or carries it away to a comfortable dining area. It uses its sharp beak first to pluck the feathers off the dead bird and then to rip flesh from its body.

What makes the peregrine falcon more amazing than other predatory birds? Well, its speed! This bird usually travels at about 25-31 mph. It can speed up to 70 mph when pursuing prey. Not too shabby for a bird! What is truly amazing is the fact that when free-falling toward the earth in attack mode, the peregrine falcon reaches speeds of almost 200 mph! One shocked pilot reported that while he was flying at 174 mph, an incredibly fast falcon flew past his window! Unsuspecting prey must feel as though they have been hit by a speeding train when this ferocious flier sinks in its claws.

talons: *claws*

Quick Fact

Peregrine falcons like to build nests high up on cliffs and even atop office buildings. Several organizations have set up webcams so that anyone can use the Web to find out what the falcons are up to.

What are the advantages and disadvantages of videotaping peregrine falcons? Explain your answer.

Take Note

The peregrine falcon is an incredible hunter that uses skill and speed to catch its food. Its powerful wings and daredevil antics make it the fastest bird in the world. It zooms into the #8 spot.
- What are other advantages to being fast, aside from catching food quickly? Explain your answer.

5   4   3   2   1

Even though the secretary bird only lays two or three eggs at a time, its nests can be as large as 7.9 feet in diameter.

BIRD

HEIGHT: 4 ft.

WINGSPAN: 6.5 ft.

WOW FACTOR: This leggy bird looks a lot like a stork, but it is actually related to falcons and hawks.

Even though it is an excellent flier like other birds of prey, the secretary bird prefers to hunt by walking! It puts its long stilt-like legs to good use. With its height, it has a good view of potential victims. Its lanky legs act as a defense against poisonous snakes. Those legs also act as lethal weapons. They can give a powerful kick that can easily stun or even kill small animals.

Although it has talons, the secretary bird cannot firmly grasp prey or tear meat to shreds. Once it catches a juicy treat, the secretary bird kills by either smashing the poor creature's skull with its beak or by stabbing it with its sharp rear talon. Then the bird opens its mouth wide and swallows the lifeless meal whole!

Turn the page and find out why this long-legged bird with the strange eating habits ranks #7 on our list of amazing birds.

SECRETARY BIRD

BIRD WATCH

The secretary bird looks very different from other birds of prey. With its extremely long legs, this bird can be up to 4.6 feet tall. Since half of its legs are covered in black feathers, it looks like it's wearing shorts. Its body is covered in white and gray feathers, while its wings and tail feathers are black. This, along with the yellow and orange skin around its eyes and long black feathers flowing from its head, makes the secretary bird one strange-looking creature!

WHAT'S FOR DINNER?

This bird eats insects, lizards, small birds, eggs, hares, rodents, and even tortoises. It also enjoys a tasty snake. Even some of the deadliest snakes, such as cobras and adders, can find themselves on the menu.

hares: *small mammals similar to rabbits*

? What are the advantages and disadvantages of hunting poisonous snakes?

FLIGHT ZONE

The secretary bird is not a globetrotter. It can only be found in Africa, south of the Sahara, where it lives in savannas. This bird prefers open fields and light, tall grass to thick jungles. The secretary bird spends its nights sleeping in flat-topped acacia trees. Every morning it flies to the ground where it spends the day hunting for prey. A secretary bird will walk 18 miles or more each day in search of food. During the hottest hours of the day, it can often be found resting in the shade of a tree.

savannas: *tropical or subtropical grasslands*

The Expert Says...

" The diet of the secretary bird is made up of virtually anything it can find and kill … its cavernous gape allows it to swallow quite large items whole … in one case of mistaken identity one bird swallowed a driven golf ball. "

— Peter Steyn, author of *Birds of Prey of Southern Africa*

gape: *open mouth*

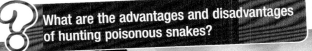

It can get hot on the savanna! This secretary bird takes a refreshing drink.

? Why is it dangerous for a secretary bird to swallow anything it comes across?

Quick Fact

Scientific studies have confirmed that the secretary bird is in some ways related to falcons and hawks. However, this bird of prey is so unusual that scientists have classified it in a family by itself!

family: *group of things that are alike*

SNAKES AND LADDERS

Check out the steps below to see how the secretary bird deals with deadly snakes!

STEP 1

The secretary bird spreads its wings and drops its tail feathers between its legs. These large moving targets confuse the snake.

STEP 2

Rather than risking a lethal bite to its face or body, the tall bird stomps its victim to unconsciousness with its powerful legs! The scales on its legs protect it from the snake's bites.

STEP 3

The secretary bird is extremely accurate in its movements. It is able to stab a moving snake in the skull with its talons or beak!

STEP 4

Dinner is served!

Quick Fact

The secretary bird's name may have come from the Arabic word *saqr-et-tair*, which means hunter-bird. A more popular story, however, is that the bird was named after 19th century secretaries. These men wore gray tailcoats and knee-length pants called knickerbockers. They carried goose-quill pens tucked behind their ears — an outfit that looked like the feathers of the secretary bird.

Take Note

The secretary bird strolls into the #7 spot. It does not have the peregrine falcon's speed, nor does it travel as far as the sooty shearwater. But it is so unusual it is in a class of its own. Plus, its hunting style is unique. It is one of the only birds that hunts on foot, and hunts prey too deadly for other predators.

- Compare the hunting strategies of the secretary bird and the peregrine falcon. Which do you find more amazing? Why?

5   4   3   2   1

The hornbill's head gets its color from a gland that produces a yellow oil. The pigment rubs off on the hands of keepers when the bird is touched.

BILL

LENGTH: 3.3 to 4 ft.

WINGSPAN: 3.3 to 5 ft.

WOW FACTOR: Its appearance and nesting habits make the great hornbill a unique bird.

The great hornbill is certainly interesting looking! The brightly colored casque on top of the hornbill's head serves many purposes. During mating season, males compete in casque-butting contests for females. The victor of these head-on collisions gets the mate, while the loser gets nothing but a splitting headache!

However, appearance isn't the only trait that makes this bird amazing. The great hornbill helps plants grow and also participates in one of the most interesting breeding processes in the bird world.

When the female lays her egg, she, with the help of her mate, encloses herself in a hollow tree using mud and dung. Only a small hole remains so that the male can bring food to her. The female can be locked in this tree for up to four months until her baby is almost ready to leave the nest. A week before the baby is ready to leave the shelter, the female frees herself and helps the male in finding food to feed their baby.

Read on to find out more about the unusual activities of this unmistakable bird.

casque: *helmet-shaped formation on the head*

GREAT HORNBILL

BIRD WATCH

The largest of the hornbill family, the great hornbill has a black body with white tips on its flight feathers, a white neck, and white stripes on its tail feathers. It has a curved bill and a golden casque on its head. Although it looks heavy, the casque is actually very light. It's made of thin, hollow bones.

Quick Fact

It may be funny-looking, but the hornbill's casque can do some amazing things. When the hornbill calls, sounds vibrate inside the casque, which makes the call sound even louder. The casque also lets other hornbills know when the bird is old enough to mate. It takes five years for the casque to fully develop.

The great hornbill loves fruit such as the papaya. It is also able to consume as many as 150 figs in one meal.

WHAT'S FOR DINNER?

Primarily a fruit eater, the great hornbill is also known to eat insects, snakes, lizards, and small mammals. Its diet also depends on where it lives. For instance, in India, hornbills primarily eat figs.

Hornbills play an important role in conserving the forest. The undigested seeds of the fruit they eat are spread throughout the forest in their droppings, transporting the seeds to a new area and helping more plants grow.

Why is it important for hornbills and other birds to help in conserving the forest? What would happen if birds didn't excrete seeds?

FLIGHT ZONE

This large bird favors hot climates. It can be found in India, Indonesia, Malaysia, and southeastern China. It seeks shelter in evergreen and moist forests and jungles in the Himalayan foothills and lowland plains.

The Expert Says...

" Everything about this beautifully plumaged but bizarre creature makes it worthy of a place on a list of amazing birds. In addition to all the features listed above, the stiff flight feathers make a loud 'whooshing' sound in flight. They're often very difficult to see — I've never seen one — but you'll know they're about when one flies high above the tall forest canopy. "

— Ian A. McLaren, Ph.D., Professor Emeritus, Biology Department, Dalhousie University

canopy: *top layer of a forest*

THE BIZARRE NESTING HABITS OF THE HORNBILL

A newspaper article from *The Gazette*
By David Bird, April 24, 1993

... Most pairs of hornbills select a natural hole in a tree or rock face for a nest site. The entrance is sealed up with mud, leaving a vertical slit, with the female doing most of this work. The hole is left just large enough for the female to squeeze herself in. ...

Why do they do this? Apparently, the sealed nest protects Mom and the kids from predators. There is even a long "funk hole" above them into which they can crawl out of reach of any predators with long arms. ...

While Mom stays inside with the chicks, the male busies itself bringing in the groceries. For example, the male silvery-cheeked hornbill makes 1,600 deliveries of food over a season, each time carrying an average of 15 fruits.

During courtship, the male brings the female food. This reassures the female that the male will feed her while she is sealed up in the nest with the chicks.

You can well imagine that nest hygiene might be a little important in such closed quarters. Indeed it is. Both the female and the chicks lift their rear ends up to the slit to squirt out their droppings. Even food remains and debris are chucked out.

In some cases, the female leaves the nest before the chicks. When this happens, the chicks reseal the cavity with their own droppings to keep out predators.

There is still much to be learned about hornbills. The conservation ecology of the great hornbill is currently being studied in the mountains of southwestern India. Apparently, fig trees figure big in their lifestyle. When other trees are without fruit, the fig trees sustain the great hornbills.

---

hygiene: *cleanliness*
debris: *garbage*
cavity: *hole*
conservation ecology: *protection of living things and their environment*

Take Note

The secretary bird and the great hornbill both have unusual appearances and exhibit what may be considered strange behavior. However, the hornbill's fascinating breeding habits and its importance in conserving the forest put this bird higher on our list. It is ranked #6.

- There are many benefits and drawbacks to the hornbill's unique nesting strategy. What are the pros and cons? Which other birds would benefit from this lifestyle?

This Egyptian vulture has managed to crack open the biggest bird egg in the world — an ostrich egg!

TURE

LENGTH: 2 to 2.3 ft.

WINGSPAN: 5 to 6 ft.

WOW FACTOR: This bird is clever enough to use tools, but just how smart can it be? After all, it eats animal dung and roadkill.

Have you ever heard the saying "One person's trash is another person's treasure"? Well, that is certainly true in the case of the Egyptian vulture. Like all vultures, this scavenger thrives on the animal carcasses left behind by predators such as lions and hyenas. Egyptian vultures also love to eat all sorts of garbage. The best place to find garbage is in towns and villages where people live. Vultures are not shy birds and are comfortable living near humans to feed on their garbage.

It doesn't limit itself to dead animals though. A brainy bird, the Egyptian vulture has developed a unique skill that allows it to chow down on the largest bird on Earth. Okay, so the vulture doesn't actually eat a full-grown ostrich, but it does eat ostrich eggs.

Not only does this hungry bird eat eggs and dead animals, but it also loves the taste of animal dung! Apparently, certain dung has nutrients that help the Egyptian vulture maintain its attractive features.

Have we made you hungry yet? Probably not, but keep reading about this interesting bird.

scavenger: *animal that feeds on dead matter*
carcasses: *dead bodies*

EGYPTIAN VULTURE

BIRD WATCH

The Egyptian vulture is the smallest of the European vultures. Most of its body is white with black wing and tail tips. Egyptian vultures can also be dark depending on where they live. Its legs and talons are pink, and its face is yellow and featherless. Because of the dung they eat, these birds maintain a yellow complexion.

WHAT'S FOR DINNER?

The Egyptian vulture feasts on dead and rotting meat! But carcasses aren't its only food source. This bird will also eat insects, small animals, decaying fruits and vegetables, and garbage. It also enjoys the dung of large animals, especially lions. Egyptian vultures snack on eggs, especially ostrich eggs. These eggs are too large and strong for the vulture to break open with its beak, but it has found a handy solution to that problem! The vulture grasps a stone firmly in its beak and hurls it at the egg. It does this repeatedly until the egg finally cracks open. Then it gets to enjoy the slimy goo inside.

The Expert Says...

" I think the most amazing behavior exhibited by the Egyptian vulture is their ability to use tools to break open ostrich eggs. … an Egyptian vulture … had flown off course during a show. … He was dropping rocks on the shiny metal tracks just as he would drop rocks to break open an egg. His natural behavior of using tools actually helped us to find him. "

— Jim Nemet, Senior Education Specialist, Cleveland Metroparks Zoo

FLIGHT ZONE

Its name may lead you to believe that this bird can only be found in Egypt. In reality, the Egyptian vulture has a vast range and can be found in Africa, India, the Middle East, and southern Europe. It lives in open plains, savannas, mountainous and coastal areas, and villages.

Quick Fact

The Egyptian vulture is also known as the "Pharaoh's Chicken." It got this name when an Egyptian pharaoh made a law that said anyone who killed an Egyptian vulture would be put to death. The pharaoh thought that the essential task these birds performed by eating rotting meat was too important to risk losing them.

? What would happen if vultures did not eat carcasses and they were left to rot in the sun?

This clever Egyptian vulture uses a stone to break open an ostrich egg.

? Think like an ornithologist and try to explain how it's possible that Egyptian vultures have evolved to use tools, while other vultures have not.

IT'S GREAT TO BE GROSS — VULTURES HAVE FUN

A magazine article from
Ranger Rick, October 2001
By Claire Miller

It's true — vultures look weird and sometimes they're kind of gross. But just look at all the amazing things they do!

If you think vultures eat rotten stuff, you're dead right! They're famous for gobbling down meat that is decaying and smells really awful.

Most creatures would get sick or die if they ate what vultures eat. But vultures have chemicals in their stomachs that protect them from the germs in their yucky food.

Vultures usually don't kill their own food — they wait for other animals (or cars) to do that. And many kinds of vultures have weak beaks, so they let other animals tear through the tough skin of a dead creature. If the meat gets rotten while they wait, that's okay. It's still just right for a vulture. *Mmmm!* …

Watch a flock of vultures gliding quietly in circles above you, and you'll be amazed. They swirl around and around and rise higher and higher on warm air currents. They can soar for hours without flapping their wings. They may rise so high that they become tiny specks and then disappear in the sky. But when they're hungry, they fly near the ground. They want to be first on the scene when an animal dies! …

An Egyptian vulture feeds on an antelope carcass.

Take Note

The Egyptian vulture is #5 on our list because it is one of the only animals in the world that routinely uses tools. As a scavenger, it eats things that would make many animals sick. In doing so, it provides an important service by preventing the growth of deadly bacteria and helping to halt the spread of disease.

- Share your thoughts on this ranking, considering the unique characteristics of the previous birds on the list. What type of features do you expect the top four birds to have?

5   4   3   2   1

4 OSTRICH

You don't have to travel to Africa to see an ostrich! Ostriches are raised on farms across the world for meat.

HEIGHT: Up to 8.5 ft.

WEIGHT: Approximately 300 lb.

WOW FACTOR: Not only is the ostrich the largest bird in the world, but it's also the fastest runner!

If you are lucky enough to go on an African safari, you might get a chance to see the largest bird in the world in its natural habitat. Don't look up in the sky or in tall trees for it though. This heavyweight keep its feet firmly planted on the ground.

The ostrich's body may be large, but its wings are downright puny. This bizarre bird does not fly, and it has an interesting way of running. It trots along on its toes, which helps the ostrich to outsprint most of its predators. Only the cheetah can run faster than this brisk bird!

With powerful legs, a long neck, and a coat of fluffy feathers, this bird stands out in a crowd. But the ostrich's appearance is only a small part of what makes it amazing. Read on to learn more about this gigantic bird.

OSTRICH

BIRD WATCH

The ostrich's large body is covered with loose, soft feathers that are unique in the bird world. Males are jet black with white plumage, while females are an earthy gray-brown. Its long neck acts like a periscope, giving the bird an excellent view of its surroundings. Ostriches' legs are very powerful for many reasons. A single kick can kill predators such as lions. They also have a four-inch-long claw on each foot that they can use to defend themselves.

A single stride of a running ostrich can be up to 16 feet long! In addition, ostriches can run up to 30 mph. They have been known to reach 45 mph in short bursts, which is twice as fast as the best Olympic sprinter.

WHAT'S FOR DINNER?

The majority of the ostrich's diet is made up of vegetation, and it eats plants, fruits, seeds, and nuts. It will also eat small lizards and enjoys a tasty bug or two. Its long neck allows the ostrich to easily eat food off the ground as well as from small trees.

 Name other animals that benefit from long necks and height. How are these characteristics beneficial to survival?

NO-FLIGHT ZONE

The ostrich's habitat is limited by the fact that it can't fly. Unlike other birds that travel to many different locations, the ostrich does not migrate. It makes its home in the dry savannas and deserts of central and southern Africa.

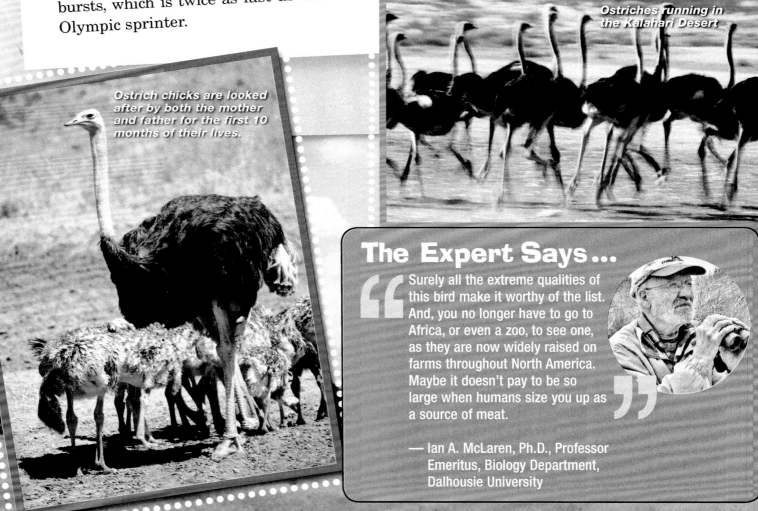

Ostriches running in the Kalahari Desert

Ostrich chicks are looked after by both the mother and father for the first 10 months of their lives.

The Expert Says...

" Surely all the extreme qualities of this bird make it worthy of the list. And, you no longer have to go to Africa, or even a zoo, to see one, as they are now widely raised on farms throughout North America. Maybe it doesn't pay to be so large when humans size you up as a source of meat. "

— Ian A. McLaren, Ph.D., Professor Emeritus, Biology Department, Dalhousie University

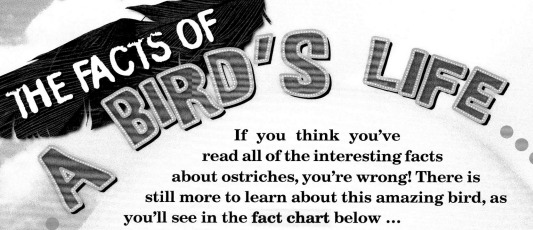

THE FACTS OF A BIRD'S LIFE

If you think you've read all of the interesting facts about ostriches, you're wrong! There is still more to learn about this amazing bird, as you'll see in the **fact chart** below ...

Ostriches lay the largest eggs in the bird world, weighing over two pounds each. The eggs are so strong that a person can stand on one without breaking it. One egg is the equivalent of 24 chicken eggs and takes about two hours to boil!

Ostriches are one of the longest living birds, surviving for up to 70 years.

A common myth about ostriches is that when they are frightened they bury their heads in the ground. This rumor may have started because of an interesting technique ostriches occasionally use to avoid being eaten. When it can't run away from danger, an ostrich will lie down with its head and neck stretched out on the sand. Its beige head and neck blend into the surroundings and seem to disappear, while its motionless body looks like a rock or a pile of dirt.

It's not often that the ostrich stretches out its wings, but when it does, it's for two simple reasons. First, when it's running quickly, it will stretch out its wings for balance, especially when changing directions. Second, during courtship the ostrich stretches out its wings and tail feathers to show dominance.

Ostriches do not need to drink water because they get enough from the plants they eat. They are also able to raise their body temperatures on hot days to prevent water loss.

A fully-grown ostrich weighs between 150 and 330 pounds.

Quick Fact

An ostrich's eye is almost two inches across, making it the largest eye of any land animal.

Take Note

The ostrich certainly is extraordinary! It is the largest bird in the world, with the largest eyes, the longest neck, and the largest eggs. It is also the fastest runner, putting it #4 on our list.
• Of all the facts you've learned about ostriches, what fact do you find the most interesting? Explain your answer.

5   4   3   2

The ruby-throated hummingbird typically beats its wings about 40 to 80 times per second. During courtship rituals it beats them up to 200 times per second!

ED HUMMINGBIRD

LENGTH: 2.8 to 3.5 in.

WINGSPAN: 3 to 4.3 in.

WOW FACTOR: Watch out! The ruby-throated hummingbird may be tiny, but it is a fast and skillful flier. Its amazing airborne acrobatics set it apart from the average bird.

Whoever says that bigger is better obviously has never met a ruby-throated hummingbird. This tiny bird weighs no more than a nickel, but it can outfly most birds.

This bird can fly backward, forward, sideways, and up and down. It can stop immediately and hover in midair. This allows the hummingbird to dodge other birds, including predatory hawks and falcons. While flying normally, the ruby-throated hummingbird usually moves at about 30 mph. When it is trying to escape a predator, it can reach speeds of approximately 50 to 62 mph.

Watching a hummingbird fly is like watching a movie on fast-forward. This bird does everything at high speed. It also has a nasty temper, starting fights with other birds over food.

Read on to learn more about this pint-sized phenomenon.

RUBY-THROATED HUMMINGBIRD

BIRD WATCH

The ruby-throated hummingbird is named after the splash of bright red feathers that cover its throat. Only the males have this trademark coloring though, which they use to attract a mate. Females have a white neck and chest and are larger than the males. This hummingbird's specially formed wings are rigid from shoulder to tip, giving it flying abilities similar to those of a helicopter.

WHAT'S FOR DINNER?

It may be tiny, but the ruby-throated hummingbird has an enormous appetite! Nectar from flowers makes up the bulk of this bird's diet. Using its needle-like beak, the bird laps up this easily digested sugar in quantities equal to 50 percent of its total body weight!

FLIGHT ZONE

This fascinating bird can be found throughout North America, east of the Mississippi River and up into southern Canada. As winter approaches, it performs a remarkable migration down to Central America, flying non-stop across the Gulf of Mexico.

? What facts about the ruby-throated hummingbird's eating habits and its physical attributes make a long trip across open water so unbelievable?

The female hummingbird only lays two eggs because it would be too hard for her to look after more than two chicks.

When hummingbird chicks hatch, they are less than an inch long!

Quick Fact

A human being with the metabolism of a hummingbird would have to eat one and a half times his or her body weight every day. That is like a 150-pound person eating 225 pounds of food each day!

metabolism: *process that breaks down food substances in the body to produce energy*

The Expert Says...

" The ruby-throated hummingbird is the smallest bird in eastern North America; you could mail eight of them with one U.S. stamp. Hummingbirds have nasty tempers — if they got as big as robins, it wouldn't be safe to go outdoors. "

— Lanny Chambers, ornithologist and creator of www.hummingbirds.net

Quick Fact

By the time a hummingbird chick can fly and is ready to leave the nest, it may weigh about 0.16 ounces. Meanwhile its poor mother, who has fed and cared for it alone, is down to only about 0.09 ounces due to the stress and added responsibility.

10   9   8   7   6

Go Ahead and Ask!

Do you have questions about hummingbirds that you wish could be answered? Don't get in a flap — you might find the answers in this fascinating Q&A!

Q How long do hummingbirds live?

A Experts believe that hummingbirds live about three to four years. But the record stands for a female who was caught and tagged in Colorado in 1976 and found in the same area again 12 years later.

Q What animals prey on hummingbirds?

A It's rare for a ruby-throated hummingbird to be caught by a predator because of its incredible speed. However, larger birds, snakes, and mammals such as cats and foxes have been known to catch one. And the hummingbird is so little that every once in a while it can get caught within a spider's web!

Q Do hummingbirds migrate?

A Certain species of hummingbird migrate. Some species have adapted to the cold climates of North America, whereas others seek warm weather all year round. These tiny marvels can travel quite a long distance, despite their size. Ornithologists have shown that ruby-throated hummingbirds can fly non-stop across the Gulf of Mexico. Most ruby-throats winter in places between southern Mexico and northern Panama.

Q How can I attract a hummingbird to my home?

A Planting a hummingbird garden full of colorful flowers filled with nectar is a great way to attract the birds. Choose plants that grow at different times throughout the spring, summer, and fall seasons. This will keep hummingbirds coming to your place most of the year. In addition, hang bird feeders filled with sugar water (which you can make at home using one part white cane sugar to four parts water). And if you find any dead insects, throw those in the feeder too; they're good protein for hummingbirds!

Take Note

The ruby-throated hummingbird is one of the smallest birds in the world, with the fewest feathers of any bird, the highest metabolism, and the most unique flying ability. The habits and migratory pattern of this tiny marvel are incredible, making this impressive little bird #3.

• What are two or three more questions you have about ruby-throated hummingbirds? Why would you ask these questions?

5 4 **3** 2 1

This unique bird is officially considered an endangered species. Only 1,200 to 1,500 cassowaries are alive today.

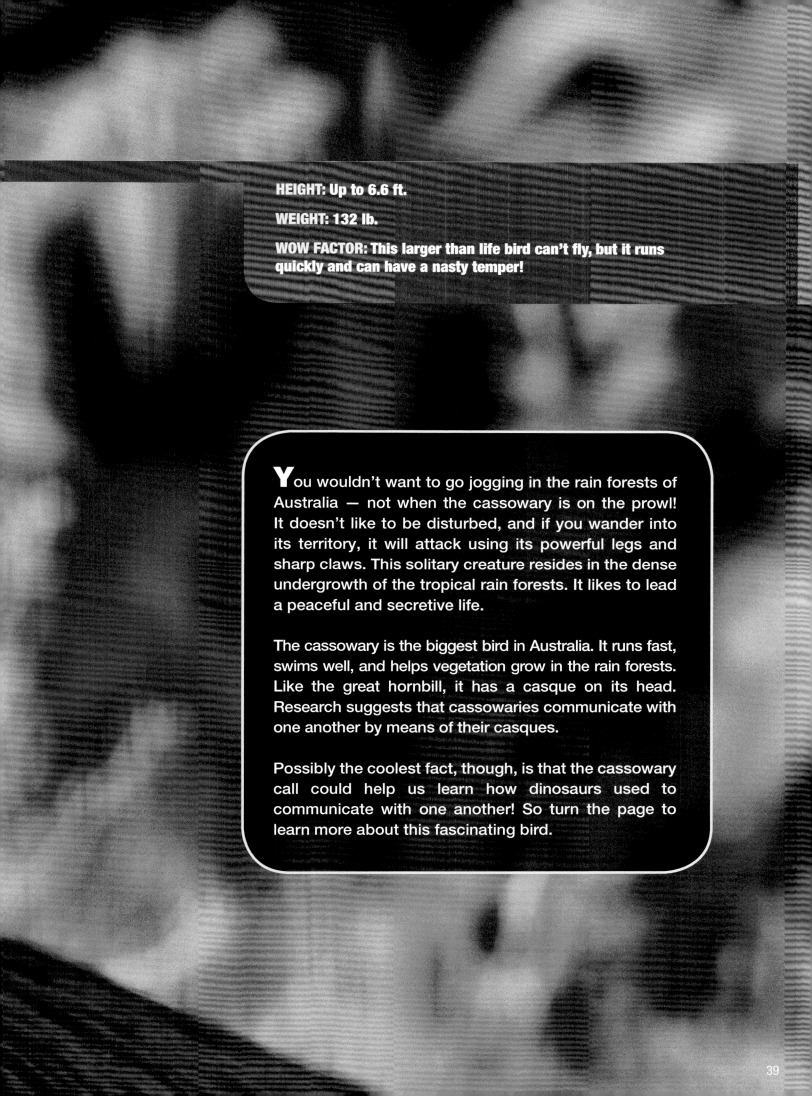

HEIGHT: Up to 6.6 ft.

WEIGHT: 132 lb.

WOW FACTOR: This larger than life bird can't fly, but it runs quickly and can have a nasty temper!

You wouldn't want to go jogging in the rain forests of Australia — not when the cassowary is on the prowl! It doesn't like to be disturbed, and if you wander into its territory, it will attack using its powerful legs and sharp claws. This solitary creature resides in the dense undergrowth of the tropical rain forests. It likes to lead a peaceful and secretive life.

The cassowary is the biggest bird in Australia. It runs fast, swims well, and helps vegetation grow in the rain forests. Like the great hornbill, it has a casque on its head. Research suggests that cassowaries communicate with one another by means of their casques.

Possibly the coolest fact, though, is that the cassowary call could help us learn how dinosaurs used to communicate with one another! So turn the page to learn more about this fascinating bird.

CASSOWARY

BIRD WATCH

The cassowary's tiny wings are hidden beneath a thick coat of glossy, black feathers. Its long neck and head are a bright mixture of reds and blues, and it has a tall casque on top of its head. Females are bigger and more brightly colored. Cassowaries have long, powerful legs with three-toed feet. Each foot has a razor-sharp claw that's four and a half inches long. Even though the cassowary can't fly, it is a powerful swimmer and a fast runner. Its strong legs enable it to reach speeds of up to 31 mph and jump as high as five feet.

WHAT'S FOR DINNER?

Cassowaries eat about 150 different types of forest fruits, which make up 90 percent of their diet. Their favorite snack is the appropriately named cassowary plum, a large fruit with blue skin. While this plum is poisonous to us, these big birds thrive on them. Cassowaries will also eat fungi, insects, frogs, snakes, and other small animals. Cassowaries mostly eat fruit, and the seeds in their dung help plants grow and produce more fruit.

NO-FLIGHT ZONE

The elusive cassowary can only be found in Australia and Papua New Guinea. It favors the dense tropical rain forests native to this area. A solitary bird, it likes the shelter of rain forests and swampy areas. Unfortunately, much of the cassowaries' habitat has been cleared by people to build homes and businesses. This is leading to a significant decrease in the cassowary population.

elusive: *hard to find*

Quick Fact

Typically a shy bird, the cassowary can become violent if approached. Over 220 attacks on humans have been recorded. According to records, only one person has ever died after being attacked by a cassowary.

? What aspect of cassowary behavior, combined with its choice of habitat, makes it difficult to say for certain that only one person has ever died as the result of an attack?

The cassowary can build a layer of fat on its back large enough to sustain it for nearly two months when food is scarce.

The Expert Says...

" … Many dinosaur fossils exhibit casques at least superficially similar to those of living cassowaries. No one knows for sure what purpose these served in these dinosaurs, so further study of living cassowaries might provide clues to how dinosaurs communicated. "

— Andrew Mack, conservation biologist, Wildlife Conservation Society

? Why do you think it's important for scientists to learn more about dinosaurs? How can the cassowary help in this research?

10   9

DOES RAIN FOREST BIRD "BOOM" LIKE A DINOSAUR?

An article from *National Geographic News*
By James Owen, November 4, 2003

It's like looking in a mirror! Compare this cassowary to the parasaurolophus dinosaur (right).

From deep in the rain forest comes a low, booming sound. It rumbles on for several minutes; enough time for any listeners to wonder whether they've stumbled into some real-life Jurassic Park. Far-fetched? Not according to scientists who've been investigating the noise. They say it could hark [recall] back to the time of the dinosaurs.

Biologists from the New York-based Wildlife Conservation Society recorded these rumbles in the jungle during a recent study of the cassowary. …

Analysis of the bird's vocalizations revealed that it has the world's lowest known birdcall. Furthermore, the research team says the cassowary could hold the key to understanding how dinosaurs communicated. …

The southern cassowary produced frequencies down to 32 hertz, while its smaller cousin, the dwarf cassowary, went even lower, dropping to a scarcely audible 23 hertz. (Humans can hear sounds with a frequency from 20 to 20,000 hertz.) …

vocalizations: *sounds made for communication*
frequencies: *numbers of wave or sound vibrations per second, measured in hertz (low hertz = deep sounds like a booming bass)*

Scientists believe cassowaries emit [send out] these low frequency vocalizations in order to communicate in dense rain forests. The distinctive call carries great distances as its long wavelength can penetrate vegetation. …

How cassowaries produce their deep "boom" is unclear, though [Andrew] Mack and his team speculate that cassowary communication is linked to the tall casques, or horn-like crests, that rise from the bird's head.

Meanwhile, that unsettling sensation produced by the cassowary's call could be the closest we'll ever get to the experience of hearing the sound of a dinosaur.

speculate: *think*

Take Note

The cassowary is #2 on our list. Although the hummingbird does everything fast, the cassowary is the largest bird in the rain forest and produces some of the lowest vocalizations of any bird. These sounds will help scientists to learn more about how dinosaurs used to communicate with one another.
• Research information about rain forests. What are the negative results of clearing away these tropical forests? What can you do to help stop the removal of rain forests?

5   4   3   **2**   1

The emperor penguin must move slowly on land or it will overheat. Its feathers and a thick layer of fat provide remarkable insulation against the incredibly cold weather.

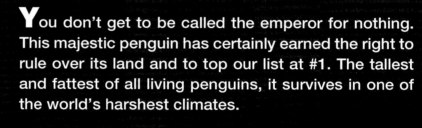

HEIGHT: About 3.5 ft.

WEIGHT: Up to 88 lb.

WOW FACTOR: Life is hard for this bird. Luckily, the emperor penguin is perfectly equipped to survive in its harsh habitat.

You don't get to be called the emperor for nothing. This majestic penguin has certainly earned the right to rule over its land and to top our list at #1. The tallest and fattest of all living penguins, it survives in one of the world's harshest climates.

Spending half of its life in perpetual darkness, this large bird breeds in one of the coldest climates in the world. It can survive for months without eating. It travels across vast distances in search of food, plunging into frigid waters that would kill a human.

Unlike most birds that breed in the spring, emperor penguins reproduce during the wintertime. They do this because by the time the babies are born and ready to migrate, the temperatures are warmer and more forgiving. While males are incubating the eggs, the temperatures are so cold that they huddle together for warmth. Males take turns circling in and out of the center of the huddle, which can be as much as 20 degrees warmer!

Read on to discover the emperor penguin's secrets for survival in the barren land it calls home.

perpetual: *occurring continually*
incubating: *to sit on eggs to hatch them by warmth*

EMPEROR PENGUIN

BIRD WATCH

The majestic emperor penguin is always ready for a formal function! Its wings and back are blackish-blue and its stomach is yellowish-white. Its black head is highlighted by yellow and white patches that extend down its neck. Its stiff wings look more like flippers and are used to propel this excellent swimmer through the chilly waters where it hunts.

If emperor penguins can't fly and are great swimmers, why do you think they are classified as birds?

WHAT'S FOR DINNER?

Because it is so cold on the Antarctic continent, very little vegetation grows. So it is not surprising that these skilled swimmers rely on the ocean to provide their dinner. Emperor penguins dive beneath the sea ice to catch fish, shellfish, and squid.

NO-FLIGHT ZONE

Emperor penguins can be found in the icy cold temperatures of Antarctica. Not many creatures can live in this frigid climate, but emperor penguins are equipped with many layers of feathers and fat to keep them warm.

Quick Fact

Despite spending a lot of time in the water, the emperor penguin never gets wet! Its oily feathers act like a wetsuit, keeping the bird's skin warm and dry.

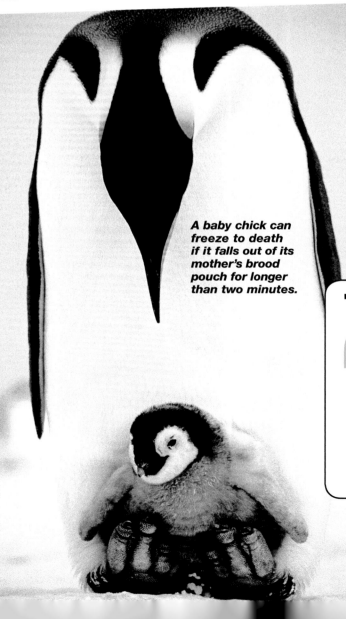

A baby chick can freeze to death if it falls out of its mother's brood pouch for longer than two minutes.

The Expert Says...

This is an animal that does things in extremes. Emperors can fast for extreme amounts of time and dive to extreme depths, which allows them to live in a very extreme place.

— Paul Ponganis, research physiologist, The Scripps Institute of Oceanography

Paul Ponganis mentioned how emperors "dive to extreme depths." How is this trait important in terms of where emperors live?

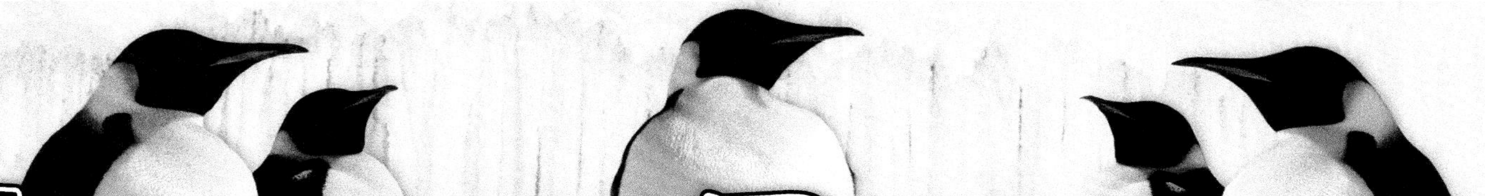

EMPEROR PENGUINS BY THE NUMBERS...

Emperor penguins are intriguing birds. Read the fact chart below to learn more about these cuddly creatures!

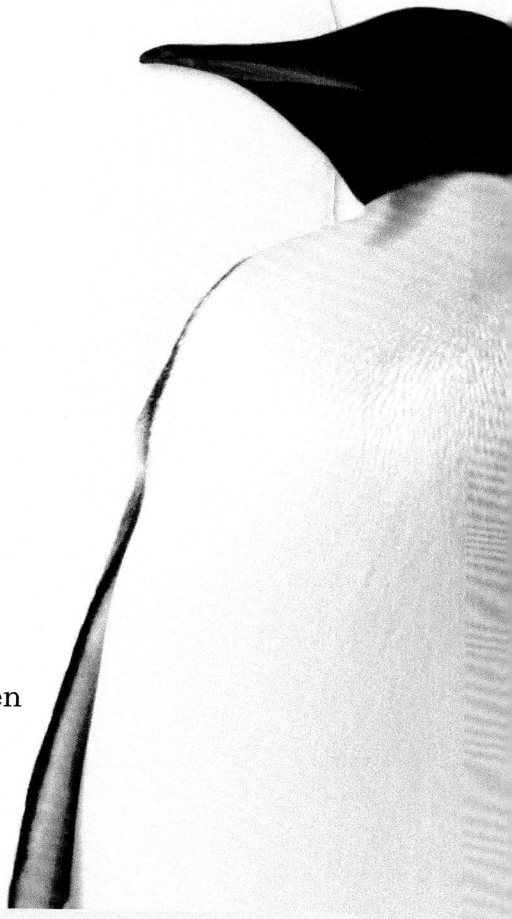

5 MPH — The speed that penguins can reach by sliding on their bellies.

20 — The number of minutes that an emperor penguin can stay underwater.

50 — The number of miles females travel to feed after they have laid their eggs.

50% — The amount of body weight an emperor can lose while incubating the egg while the female is out feeding.

60 — The number of heartbeats emperor penguins experience per minute while swimming. Typically, their hearts beat 180 to 200 times per minute while on land.

Find out how an emperor penguin's heartbeat is different from a human's heartbeat while swimming.

95°F — The temperature an emperor penguin can heat up to (even on the coldest days), thanks to its body fat and feathers.

100 — The number of miles penguins will travel when migrating from their feeding grounds to breeding grounds.

1,180 — The number of miles penguins have traveled in search of food.

1,640 — The depth in feet at which emperor penguins have been recorded diving.

10,000 — The number of penguin couples that have gathered at one specific breeding site.

Take Note

Living in such extreme conditions earns the emperor penguin the #1 spot on our list. The cassowary may be big and provide a lethal kick, but it could never live in the harsh conditions in which the emperor penguin lives.

• What more would you like to learn about emperor penguins, or any other bird on this list? What did you learn about birds that you never knew before?

5   4   3   2   1

We Thought …

Here are the criteria we used in ranking the 10 most amazing birds.

The bird:
- Eats bizarre foods
- Is an incredible swimmer
- Lives in extremely cold environments
- Can fly, but chooses not to
- Is a very fast runner
- Has strange breeding habits
- Migrates for warmer climates
- Flies at incredible speeds
- Is slowly losing its habitat

What Do You Think?

1. Do you agree with our ranking? If you don't, try ranking these birds yourself. Justify your ranking with data from your own research and reasoning. You may refer to our criteria, or you may want to draw up your own list of criteria.

2. Here are three other birds that we considered but in the end did not include in our top 10 list: the bee eater, honeyguide, and roadrunner.
   • Find out more about these birds. Do you think they should have made our list? Give reasons for your response.
   • Are there other birds that you think should have made our list? Explain your choices.

Index

A

Africa, 20, 28, 30–32
Alaska, 12–13
Antarctica, 16, 44
Arctic tern, 11–12
Australia, 39–40

B

Beak, 5, 7–9, 17, 19, 21, 28–29, 36
Brader, Kathy, 8
Breed, 11, 13, 16, 23, 25, 43, 45–46

C

California, 12–13
Canada, 36
Casque, 23–24, 39–41
Cassowary, 38–41, 45
Central America, 36
Cheetah, 31
Chicks, 9, 25, 32, 36
China, 24
Chile, 12–13
Claws, 9, 17, 39
Colorado, 37
Coniferous forests, 8
Conservation ecology, 25
Courtship, 25, 33–34

D

Diet, 8, 16, 20, 24, 32, 36, 40
Dinosaurs, 39–41

E

Eggs, 8–9, 18, 20, 27–28, 33, 36, 43, 45
Egyptian vulture, 26–29
Emperor penguin, 42–45
Endangered Species List, 16
Europe, 28
Extinction, 16
Eyesight, 7, 15–16

F

Feathers, 7–8, 11–12, 16–17, 20–21, 24, 28, 31–33, 36, 40, 42, 44–45
Fruits, 8, 25, 28, 32, 40

G

Great hornbill, 22–25, 39

H

Habitat, 5, 7–8, 31–32, 38, 40, 43, 45
Hawks, 20, 35
Helmet, 16, 23, 40
Hummingbird, 34–37, 41

I

Iceland, 16
India, 24–25, 28
Indonesia, 24
Insects, 8, 15–16, 20, 24, 28, 37, 40

J

Japan, 12–13
Jungles, 20, 24

K

Kiwi, 6–9

L

Lions, 27–28, 32

M

Mack, Andrew, 40
Malaysia, 24
Mammal, 7–8, 16, 24, 37
McLaren, Ian A., 24, 32
Meat, 15, 19, 28–29, 32
Mexico, 37
Middle East, 28
Migration, 11–13, 36, 46
Mississippi River, 36

N

Nemet, Jim, 28
Nest, 7, 11–12, 17–18, 23, 25–26, 36
New Zealand, 7–8, 12–13, 16
North America, 32, 36–37
North Island, 6–9

O

Ornithologist, 5, 11, 16, 28, 36–37
Ostrich, 9, 26–28, 30–33

P

Pacific Ocean, 10, 13
Panama, 37
Papua New Guinea, 40
Peregrine falcon, 14–17, 21
Plumage, 8, 24, 32
Ponganis, Paul, 44
Predator, 16, 25, 27, 31–32, 35, 45
Predatory birds, 8, 17
Prey, 12, 15–17, 19–21
Prowl, 16, 39

R

Rain forests, 39–41
Roadkill, 27
Rodents, 20

S

Seafood, 12
Secretary bird, 18–21, 25
Shaffer, Scott, 12
Snakes, 19–21, 24, 37, 40
Sooty shearwater, 10–13, 16, 21
Speed, 15, 17, 21, 31, 35, 40, 45–46
Squid, 12, 44
Steyn, Peter, 20

T

Talons, 15, 17, 19, 21, 28
Trefry, Phil, 16

V

Victim, 15, 17, 19, 21
Vocalizations, 41

W

Wildlife Conservation Society, 40–41